W9-ARG-838

ASSESSING MEDIA EDUCATION

LEA'S COMMUNICATION SERIES
Jennings Bryant / Dolf Zillmann, General Editors

Selected titles in media administration (William G. Christ, advisor) include:

Blanchard/Christ • *Media Education and the Liberal Arts: A Blueprint for the Profession*

Christ • Assessing *Media Education: A Resource Handbook for Educators and Administrators*

Christ • *Assessing Communication Education: A Handbook for Media, Speech, and Theatre Educators*

Christ • *Leadership in Times of Change: A Handbook for Communication and Media Administrators*

Dickson • *Mass Media Education in Transition: Preparing for the 21st Century*

For a complete list of titles in LEA's Communication Series, please contact Lawrence Erlbaum Associates, Publishers at www.erlbaum.com

ASSESSING MEDIA EDUCATION

A Resource Handbook
for Educators and Administrators

COMPONENT 3:
DEVELOPING AN ASSESSMENT PLAN

Edited by

William G. Christ
Trinity University

WITHDRAWN

TOURO COLLEGE LIBRARY
Kings Hwy

 LAWRENCE ERLBAUM ASSOCIATES, PUBLISHERS
2007   Mahwah, New Jersey   London

KH

This volume is an abridged version of *Assessing Media Education: A Resource Handbook for Educators and Administrators*, edited by William G. Christ. Additional components and the complete volume are available from Lawrence Erlbaum Associates, Inc. at www.erlbaum.com.

Copyright © 2007 by Lawrence Erlbaum Associates, Inc.
All rights reserved. No part of this book may be reproduced in any form, by photostat, microform, retrieval system, or any other means, without prior written permission of the publisher.

Lawrence Erlbaum Associates, Inc., Publishers
10 Industrial Avenue
Mahwah, New Jersey 07430
www.erlbaum.com

Cover design by Kathryn Houghtaling

Library of Congress Cataloging-in-Publication Data

Assessing media education : a resource handbook for educators and administrators / edited by William G. Christ.
    p. cm.
Includes bibliographical references and index.
ISBN 0-8058-6094-0 (pbk. : alk. paper)
1. Mass media—Study and teaching (Higher)—Evaluation—Handbooks, manuals, etc.   I. Christ, William G.
P91.3.A853   2005
302.23'071'1—dc22   2005051015
                                                              CIP

Books published by Lawrence Erlbaum Associates are printed on acid-free paper, and their bindings are chosen for strength and durability.

Printed in the United States of America
10 9 8 7 6 5 4 3 2 1

10/19/06

Contents

Preface

Assessment is an integral part of what we do as teachers, researchers, and administrators. It can be formal or informal, systematic or haphazard, harmful or rewarding. At its best, assessment can have a transforming effect on education. At its worst, it can be used as an instrument to punish people and programs.

We are living in the age of accountability. Though calls for accountability and assessment have come and gone, the current demands for proving that students are learning seem more insistent as they become codified in educational policies. The move from asking teachers what they teach to requiring programs to show that students are learning is a paradigm shift that costs blood, sweat, and tears. It requires educators to look differently at their curricula, courses, syllabuses, and measurement mechanisms.

The purpose of this book is to provide useful information to those in higher education media programs who want to create or improve their student learning assessment strategies. This component, Part I, in the main volume, describes how to develop an assessment plan, with special emphasis on mission statements.

If assessment is here to stay, then it is important for media educators to understand and use the process so that they control their own destinies. The hope is that this book will be a useful intellectual and practical resource for media educators and administrators as they grapple with the challenges of assessment.

ACKNOWLEDGMENTS

This book has been a very rewarding collaboration. I would like to publicly acknowledge the hard work of the authors involved in this project. Working with these authors has been a true pleasure. Their care and expertise will be evident to you as you read each chapter.

Second, I would like to thank the people at Lawrence Erlbaum Associates. Linda Bathgate was a major force behind the conceptualization and execution of this book. Nadine Simms has done a great job keeping the production side of the book on track. Tina Hardy did an excellent job as copy editor. The anonymous critiques of the early prospectus by conscientious reviewers made this a stronger book. I appreciate all their hard work.

From Trinity University, I would like to thank my department and the administration for their support. Trinity is an intellectually stimulating place where educational issues dealing with teaching, courses, and curricula are vigorously debated.

On a more personal note, I would like to thank those who developed the Internet and email. This project would have taken twice as long without these new communication technologies. I would also like to thank my sons Nathan and Jonathan Christ and especially my life partner, wife, and true friend, Judith Anne Christ.

Thank you one and all.

—William G. Christ
San Antonio, Texas

Component 3
Assessing Media Education
Developing an Assessment Plan

Introduction to Component 3

The chapters in this book are part of a larger book titled *Assessing Media Education: A Resource Handbook for Educators and Administrators*. This component is designed for those who need to know how to develop an assessment plan.

1

Introduction:
Why Assessment Matters[1]

William G. Christ
Department of Communication
Trinity University

Accountability to my students meant: plan the course, show up in class, keep it moving, comment thoughtfully on papers, mentor when asked, submit grades, write recommendations—the usual packet of services. My obligation to my departmental colleagues: take on my share of core courses and administrative duties. To administrators and trustees: just don't make scenes, I guess; the thought rarely crossed my mind. My responsibility to society as a whole: I cheerfully held myself accountable for the wretched of the earth. . . .

—Ohmann (2000, p. 24)

If the programmatic assessment of student learning outcomes was universally acknowledged as being necessary, important, and positive, then it would not need to be defended. Yet, even those who accept the assessment of student learning outcomes in principle can find the job of planning, assessing, tabulating, and reporting so cumbersome and costly that they feel anger toward assessment efforts.

The assessment of student learning outcomes has become the acid test for media educators. It requires a paradigm shift in a faculty's thinking. Instead of focusing on traditional assessment "inputs" like faculty degrees, number of full-time faculty, research productivity, resources, facilities, equipment, diversity, and curriculum, a student learning ap-

---

[1]An earlier version of this chapter was in the Association of Schools of Journalism and Mass Communication *Insights* periodical.

proach to assessment focuses on "outputs." Instead of asking "what do faculty need to teach," the question becomes "what do we want students to learn?" "The question, 'What is basic about our discipline?' becomes 'What is basic about the discipline that students should learn and how do we know they have learned it?' " (Christ, McCall, Rakow, & Blanchard, 1997, p. 29).

Simply stated, faculty do assessment for either internal or external reasons. Yet, where we are in the assessment debates only makes sense within the broader context of off-campus forces impacting campuses. The first part of this chapter, therefore, outlines off-campus forces. Then, definitions are given and the two reasons are laid out.

OFF-CAMPUS FORCES

Jones, Jones, and Hargrove (2003) wrote that the first documented achievement tests can be linked to the mid-1800s when "the United States began an unprecedented effort to educate the masses" (p. 14). Janesick (2001, p. 89), who made a distinction between the testing movement (just after World War I) and the assessment movement, suggested that researchers should go back to the 1880s, "when Francis Galton, in London, administered tests to hundreds of persons to test sensory reactions and reaction times of volunteers," to understand the "big picture" of assessment. Both authors document the growth of public education after World War II and the transformative nature of the 1960s. Whereas Janesick argued that Howard Gardner's research on his theory of multiple intelligences almost "single-handedly starts the assessment movement" (p. 92), both researchers indicate the importance of the 1983 United States Department of Education's National Commission on Excellence in Education publication, "A Nation at Risk: The Imperative for Educational Reform" (1983), that "clearly situated public education as being in crisis and in need of major reform. The report used test scores as the indicator of success and the goal of schooling" (Jones et al., 2003, p. 15). The use of test scores as valid measures of excellence can be seen in the use of standardized tests like the Scholastic Assessment Test, American College Testing, and the Graduate Record Exam, and in the highly politicized "No Child Left Behind Act of 2001" (2002) legislation.

The Accountability Movement

Assessment is part of a larger accountability movement. Although it is clear from the previous discussion that accountability concerns are not new (see also Martin, Overholt, & Urban, 1976, pp. 33–41), Ohmann

(2000) has suggested that the current accountability movement grew out of three main forces in the late 1960s and early 1970s. The first "was an intense fiscal crisis of the state, brought on partly by war spending, but expressed chiefly as disillusionment with Great Society programs" (p. 28). Educational costs and expenditures had increased during the 1960s and there was concern that, as then deputy commissioner in the Office of Education Terrel H. Bell reported, "Money alone could not buy good education . . ." (p. 28).

Second, Ohmann (2000) argued that the accountability movement "was partly a counterthrust against liberatory ideas and experiments in 'open education,' that is, against the critique of schooling mounted by sixties visionaries and radicals" (p. 28). If the 1960s stood for student power, a democratization of higher education, and challenges to the educational status quo, then the rise of accountability in education could be seen as a direct challenge to these forces, suggesting to some that "traditional notions about the value of democracy and the value of the individual are ultimately at stake" (Martin et al., 1976, p. 6).

Finally, the third main force driving the accountability movement in education was a reaction against the "turmoil and disruption on the campuses; political action by students and faculty members . . . ; and mounting distrust of higher education by the public . . ." (Ohmann, 2000, p. 28). This led to "the increasing demand for colleges and universities to justify what they are doing and to disclose the effectiveness and efficiency of their operations" (McConnell, 1972, p. 200). Seen in this light, "one explanation for the failure of accountability advocates to heed objections by educators is that accountability is not primarily a pedagogical movement. It is an administrative system, and as such it is impervious to arguments which are based on educational concerns" (Martin et al., 1976, p. 32).

As the modern day accountability movement was building steam in the mid-1970s, there were a number of educators who wrote scathing critiques. Martin et al. (1976), in their critique of accountability in higher education, identified three major defects: "First, it lacks an adequate theoretical base" (p. 6). Accountability is a complex construct that is not always fully investigated and explicated by those who would use it (see Sarlos, 1973, pp. 65–81). Accountability tends to concentrate on behaviors and thus is informed by behavioral theory. Martin et al. argued that behavioral analysis limits education when they wrote, "because we believe that education has something to do with rational and critical thinking, introspection, and creativity, we believe that any view which confines itself exclusively to observable phenomena leaves out something essential both to the practice of science and to the process of education" (p. 6).

Besides the concern of a lack of an adequate theoretical base, basic questions dealing with accountability are not always answered. "For example, to contend that an individual or an institution ought to be accountable immediately brings to mind the questions: accountable to whom, for what, in what manner and under what circumstances?" (Wagner, 1989, p. 1). Other questions would include the following: Who should be held accountable (e.g., teachers, parents, school systems, school administrators, school teachers)? What does it mean to be accountable? When should accountability take place (e.g., grade level, proficiency level, every year)? What should be measured (e.g., knowledge, behavior, attitudes, values; see Part II)? How should accountability be measured (e.g., through portfolios, exit interviews, tests; see Part III)?

The second defect identified by Martin et al. (1976) was that accountability in education "lacks reassuring historical precedents. In fact, something very akin to accountability has been tried before and found wanting" (p. 6). They argued that the current push for accountability was only the most recent. Previous attempts had limited success.

"Third, its political implications are not reassuring to those among us who value either individuality or democracy" (Martin et al., 1976, p. 6). As stated previously, there are those who have argued that accountability, coming out of a business-training model, is not the best model for education. Bowers (1972) went so far as to argue that "teacher accountability is incompatible with academic freedom . . ." (p. 25).

[A]ccountability proponents could argue that despite various and sometimes conflicting interpretations of accountability there is at least general agreement about the following: (1) The quality of schools can no longer be determined simply by looking at input factors such as plant facilities, the number of volumes in the library, pupil/teacher ratios or printed curricula; rather, school performance and the quality of school programs are best understood in terms of results and output, what children do or do not learn over a given period; (2) learning can be measured against costs for a specified interval as an indication of cost-effectiveness; (3) taxpayers, parents and supportive government agencies have a "right" to know about these results and the cost/benefits associated with their schools; and (4) accountability can provide this information and act as a stimulus to better school performance. (Wagner, 1989, p. 2)

Whatever the historical roots of or problems with the current accountability and assessment movements, accountability and assessment appear here to stay. (For an overview of the assessment in higher education, see Rosenbaum, 1994.)

Forces Impacting Media Education

In the late 1980s and early 1990s, as the assessment movement continued to pick up steam (see Ervin, 1988; Ewell, Hutchings, & Marchese, 1991), at least three other challenges faced media education: calls for the reinvention of undergraduate education, the convergence of communication technologies, and the philosophical and theoretical ferment in the communication field (Blanchard & Christ, 1993; Dickson, 1995; Duncan, Caywood, & Newsom, 1993; "Planning for Curricular Change," 1984, 1987; Wartella, 1994).

It was argued that the reinvention of undergraduate education called for a "New Liberal Arts" that combined elements from both traditional and newer fields and disciplines (Blanchard & Christ, 1993). There were calls for a renewed commitment from media programs to the nonmajor, general student; a call for the centrality of media studies in the common curriculum of all students. As people debated what should be the outcome of an undergraduate education (see Association of American Colleges, 1985; Boyer, 1987; "Strengthening the Ties," 1988), media educators were faced with the following questions: What does my program have to offer the general university student? If one of the outcomes of a university education is to be media literate, then what should we teach and what should students learn? (see Christ & Potter, 1998).

The convergence of communication technologies and the philosophical and theoretical ferment in the communication field suggested there needed to be a new way of looking at the major. Some went so far as to demand a "New Professionalism" that educated students to become broad-based communication practitioners (Blanchard & Christ, 1993; see "Planning for Curricular Change," 1984, 1987). The calls for a broad approach to communication and media education has been both supported and attacked (see Dickson, 1995, 2000; Duncan et al., 1993; Medsger, 1996). The point is that the convergence of technologies and the philosophical and theoretical ferment in the field required media educators to reevaluate their programs to determine if what they offered made sense philosophically, pedagogically, and practically.

Overlaid on these three challenges was the assessment movement. As stated earlier, assessment, as part of the accountability movement, has been part of higher education for over 35 years. What is different now is the intensity of the current debate, where accrediting agencies seem to be taking the student learning assessment part of their charge very seriously and where legislators are willing to link funding to results. Assessment continues to be both a promise and a plague for programs as educators grapple with high expectations and limited resources (see Christ & Blanchard, 1994).

Student Learning

A report by the Kellogg Commission on the Future of State and Land-Grant Universities (1997) demonstrates how assessment dovetails with current calls for college and university reforms. The Kellogg Commission (1997) wanted to turn schools into learning institutions. They suggested "three broad ideals":

> (1) Our institutions must become *genuine learning communities*, supporting and inspiring faculty, staff, and learners of all kinds. (2) Our learning communities should be *student centered*, committed to excellence in teaching and to meeting the legitimate needs of learners, wherever they are, whatever they need, whenever they need it. (3) Our learning communities should emphasize the importance of *a healthy learning environment* that provides students, faculty, and staff with the facilities, support, and resources they need to make this vision a reality. (pp. v–vi, italics in original)

The move from universities being conceptualized as *teaching* institutions to *learning* institutions has profound implications for higher education (cf. Christ, 1994, 1997). As universities become more focused on student learning than on teaching, more concerned with the outcomes of education than the inputs into education, then at least two things become evident. First, outcomes assessment of learning becomes a "logical" important "next step" in the process, and second, the classroom is seen as only one part, and sometimes one small part, of the total learning environment.

The shift from teaching to learning communities, from teacher-centered to student-centered approaches to education, changes the role of the classroom teacher. If, as the Kellogg Commission (1997) suggested, learning communities should be committed "to meeting the legitimate needs of learners, wherever they are, whatever they need, whenever they need it" (pp. v–vi), then it is clear that teaching and learning can no longer be confined to the classroom. And, as the costs of higher education have escalated, as more people lose access to traditional higher education opportunities (Council for Aid to Education, 1997), the idea of a 4-year residential university or college, where lectures are delivered in huge classrooms, may become an anachronism. Within all of these challenges, educators are asked to assess their programs and student learning.

DEFINITIONS

So what is assessment? Krendl, Warren, and Reid (1997) made an interesting distinction between assessment and evaluation in their discussion about distant learning:

> Assessment refers to any process that measures what students have learned from teaching strategies, including course-specific methods (e.g., assignments, class activities, and tests) and programmatic strategies (e.g., exit interviews or honors theses) designed to test specific content knowledge. This primary focus on academic content is a defining characteristic of student assessment. Evaluation, on the other hand, looks beyond this to examine the entire educational experience. The mesh between students' needs and their experiences during a course or program is the primary criterion in evaluation. Beyond teaching strategies, then, evaluation examines classroom interaction, the effectiveness of course/program administration, the quality of student support services, access to and quality of technical equipment, and cost-benefit analyses of distance-education programs. In short, every aspect of a distance course or program can be evaluated, whereas only students' mastery of course content is assessed (Rowntree, 1992). (p. 103)

The distinction between assessment and evaluation is useful in that it directs our attention to different levels or types of accountability. Haley and Jackson (1995) suggested a hierarchy of programmatic assessment that included four levels, where

> each level may be seen as a broader examination of the program. The four levels are: Level One—Evaluation of individual program components <peer teaching review and course evaluations>; Level Two—Perceptions and performance of graduating students <survey of seniors; senior essays; university comprehensives; departmental comprehensives; campaigns courses>; Level Three—Evaluations of key internal and external constituencies <faculty surveys; employer surveys; university alumni surveys; department graduate surveys>; and Level Four—Comprehensive program evaluation <program review; accreditation>. (p. 27)

Student learning outcomes assessment is normally positioned as a level-four programmatic evaluation. Of course, to do assessment is not easy. Morse and Santiago (2000) wrote that, "to evaluate student learning adequately, faculty must set programmatic goals, understand the profiles of students, define the desired outcomes for students and programs, develop instruments to measure those outcomes, and establish a feedback loop in which the information gained is used to effective positive change" (p. 33).

WHY ASSESSMENT?

There are two fundamental reasons for assessment. The first is external and the second is internal.

External

As mentioned earlier, demand for assessment grew out of calls for accountability. "House (1993) proposed three different types of accountability that institutions of higher education face: state- or public-controlled accountability, professional control (by professors and administrators), and consumer control" (Krendl et al., 1997, p. 109). These three types of accountability are external to the media unit and are often seen by the unit as being harmful, coercive, or irrelevant. Under these conditions, assessment, at its best, might be seen as an antidote to calls for accountability. For example, "Lombardi (1993) posits, 'To counter-attack against criticism from the public, we need to explain and teach the public what the universities do, how they do it, and why it costs so much ... The key weapon here is accounting' " (Haley & Jackson, 1995, p. 33). In other words, assessment is seen as a weapon to be used by the beleaguered unit to answer criticisms.

The first reason for doing assessment is that certain states, regional accrediting agencies, local administrators, professional accrediting groups, parents, and students have called for or mandated assessment. If state legislatures have developed carrots and sticks based on assessment and results, then that is an excellent reason why a unit would want to do assessment. If a unit wants to be either regionally or professionally accredited and it needs to evaluate its program and student learning outcome as part of the process, then this is an excellent reason for doing assessment. If an administration says to develop an assessment plan, then this, too, is an excellent reason for doing assessment. Ideally, a unit will be able to turn the often-odious chore of assessment into a well-articulated persuasive argument about needs and expectations. Hopefully, a unit will be able to transform all its hard work into a plan for how to improve what it does. And hopefully, a unit will be given the resources to help improve its program.

Internal

The second reason to do assessment is that it has the potential to make teachers, programs, and ultimately, students, better. Assessment can help a unit be self-reflective about what is done and why it is done. It can mean discovering the strengths and weaknesses of programs and the teaching and learning process. "Assessment is an integral part of what we do as teachers, researchers, and administrators. It can be formal or informal, systematic or haphazard, harmful or rewarding. At its best, assessment can have a transforming effect on education. At its worst, it can be used as an instrument to punish people and programs" (Christ, 1994, p. x).

SUMMARY

This book stresses the development of an assessment plan. In Chapters 2 and 3, the authors discuss how to develop an assessment plan and the importance of usable, descriptive mission statements. They argue that an assessment plan should link a university's mission statement with the program's mission that should confirm the program's core values, competencies, and knowledge. These core values, competencies, and knowledge should be linked to student learning outcomes which are clearly present in programs' curricula and courses and even exercises and experiences within courses. Once the student learning outcomes are articulated, then both indirect and direct methods can be developed to continually assess the outcomes. Finally, the results from the assessment should be fed back into the system.

CONCLUSION

Ultimately, there is good assessment and bad assessment. Bad assessment is when, through lack of time, resources or will, tests or measures are thrown together to appease some outside agency or administrator. Good assessment is assessment that helps teachers and programs improve what they do so that teachers can teach and students can learn better. The American Association for Higher Education (AAHE Assessment Forum, 1997) suggests nine key "principles of good practice for assessing student learning":

1. The assessment of student learning begins with educational values; 2. Assessment is most effective when it reflects an understanding of learning as multidimensional, integrated, and revealed in performance over time; 3. Assessment works best when the programs it seeks to improve have clear, explicitly stated purposes; 4. Assessment requires attention to outcomes but also and equally to the experiences that lead to those outcomes; 5. Assessment works best when it is ongoing, not episodic; 6. Assessment fosters wider improvement when representatives from across the educational community are involved; 7. Assessment makes a difference when it begins with issues of use and illuminates questions that people really care about;

8. Assessment is most likely to lead to improvement when it is part of a larger set of conditions that promote change; 9. Through assessment, educators meet responsibilities to students and to the public. (pp. 11-12)

After evaluating a trial batch of student learning assessment plans from a number of Journalism and Mass Communication programs who were coming up for accreditation, the AEJMC Teaching Standards Committee (Hansen, 2004) suggested the following:

1. Assessment plans should include the unit's mission statement.
2. Assessment plans should include the "professional values and competencies" all students must master, and plans should be revised to insure they conform to the final, approved language for the "professional values and competencies" as stated in ACEJMC's . . . Accreditation Standards.
3. Assessment plans should address the means by which students will be made aware of the "professional values and competencies" as they move through the program and the major.
4. Assessment plans should reflect the concept of different levels of student learning (awareness, understanding and application). The methods used to assess student learning should indicate the level at which students are expected to perform. For example, if a direct measure is being used to evaluate student mastery of the competency of writing correctly and clearly, the measurement method should reflect the level of performance expected (most likely "application" for that competency).
5. Assessment plans should clearly identify which methods are deemed to be direct and which are deemed to be indirect measures of student learning.
6. Assessment plans should clearly link the method for measuring student learning with the appropriate "professional values and competencies" that are expected to be measured through that method.
7. Assessment plans should address the "indicators" that are articulated in Standard 9 of the new Accrediting Standards to ensure that appropriate evidence is provided for site team visitors.
8. Assessment plans should specifically articulate how the assessment effort will be staffed and maintained so that assessment is ongoing.
9. Assessment plans should specifically detail how the data collected from the direct and indirect measures will be used to improve curriculum and instruction over time.

Assessment did not just happen. It has developed within a complex of powerful forces that have continued to impact higher education. Why assessment matters is a function of both external constituencies and internal needs. The bottom line is that it is useful for media educators to address the questions: What do we want to be able to say about our students when they graduate from our program? Why do we teach what we teach? And, for assessment purposes, how do we know our students are learning what we are teaching? Hopefully, this book will help generate a discussion that will help us answer these questions.

REFERENCES

Accrediting Council on Education in Journalism and Mass Communications. (2004). *New accrediting standards.* Retrieved July 24, 2004, from http://www.ukans.edu/~acejmc/BREAKING/New_standards_9-03.pdf

American Association for Higher Education Assessment Forum. (1997). *9 principles of good practice for assessing student learning.* Retrieved March 25, 2005, from http://www.aahe.org/assessment/principl.htm

Association of American Colleges. (1985). *Integrity in the college curriculum: A report to the academic community.* Washington, DC: Author.

Blanchard, R. O., & Christ, W. G. (1993). *Media education and the liberal arts: A blueprint for the new professionalism.* Hillsdale, NJ: Lawrence Erlbaum Associates, Inc.

Bowers, C. A. (1972). Accountability from a humanist point of view. In F. J. Sciara & R. K. Jantz (Eds.), *Accountability in American education* (pp. 25–33). Boston: Allyn & Bacon.

Boyer, E. L. (1987). *College: The undergraduate experience in America.* New York: The Carnegie Foundation for the Advancement of Teaching, Harper & Row.

Christ, W. G. (Ed.). (1994). *Assessing communication education.* Hillsdale, NJ: Lawrence Erlbaum Associates, Inc.

Christ, W. G. (Ed.). (1997). *Media education assessment handbook.* Mahwah, NJ: Lawrence Erlbaum Associates, Inc.

Christ, W. G., & Blanchard, R. O. (1994). Mission statements, outcomes and the new liberal arts. In W. G. Christ (Ed.), *Assessing communication education* (pp. 31–55). Hillsdale, NJ: Lawrence Erlbaum Associates, Inc.

Christ, W. G., McCall, J. M., Rakow, L., & Blanchard, R. O. (1997). Integrated communication programs. In W. G. Christ (Ed.), *Media education assessment handbook* (pp. 23–53). Mahwah, NJ: Lawrence Erlbaum Associates, Inc.

Christ, W. G., & Potter, W. J. (1998). Media literacy, media education, and the academy. *Journal of Communication, 48*(1), 5–15.

Council for Aid to Education. (1997). *Breaking the social contract. The fiscal crisis in higher education.* Retrieved March 25, 2005, from http://www.rand.org/publications/CAE/CAE100/index.html

Dickson, T. (1995, August). *Meeting the challenges and opportunities facing media education: A report on the findings of the AEJMC Curriculum Task Force.* Paper presented at the annual convention of the Association for Education in Journalism and Mass Communication, Washington, DC.

Dickson, T. (2000). *Mass media education in transition.* Mahwah, NJ: Lawrence Erlbaum Associates, Inc.

Duncan, T., Caywood, C., & Newsom, D. (1993, December). *Preparing advertising and public relations students for the communications industry in the 21st century.* A report of the Task Force on Integrated Curriculum.

Ervin, R. F. (1988). Outcomes assessment: The rationale and the implementation. In R. L. Hoskins (Ed.), *Insights* (pp. 19–23). Columbia, SC: Association of Schools of Journalism and Mass Communication.

Ewell, P. T., Hutchings, P., & Marchese, T. (1991). *Reprise 1991: Reprints of two papers treating assessment's history and implementation.* Washington, DC: American Association for Higher Education, Assessment Forum.

Haley, E., & Jackson, D. (1995). A conceptualization of assessment for mass communication programs. *Journalism and Mass Communication Educator, 51,* 26–34.

Hansen, K. (2004). *Accreditation guidelines for evaluating assessment of student learning plans* (Memorandum sent by the Committee on Teaching Standards chair to the chair of the Accrediting Council on Education in Journalism and Mass Communication accrediting committee).

House, E. (1993). *Professional evaluation.* Newbury Park, CA: Sage.

Janesick, V. J. (2001). *The assessment debate.* Santa Barbara, CA: AGC-CLIO, Inc.

Jones, M. G., Jones, B. D., & Hargrove, T. Y. (2003). *The unintended consequences of high-stakes testing.* Lanham, MD: Rowman & Littlefield Publishers, Inc.

Kellogg Commission on the Future of State and Land-Grant Universities. (1997). *Returning to our roots: The student experience.* Retrieved March 25, 2005, from http://www. nasulgc.org/publications/Kellogg/Kellogg2000_StudentExp.pdf

Krendl, K. A., Warren, R., & Reid, K. A. (1997). Distance learning. In W. G. Christ (Ed.), *Assessing communication education* (pp. 99–119). Mahwah, NJ: Lawrence Erlbaum Associates, Inc.

Lombardi, V. (1993). With their accounts in order, colleges can win back their critics. *The Chronicle of Higher Education, 39,* A40.

Martin, D. T., Overholt, G. E., & Urban, W. J. (1976). *Accountability in American education: A critique.* Princeton, NJ: Princeton Book Company.

McConnell, T. R. (1972). Accountability and autonomy. In F. J. Sciara & R. K. Jantz (Eds.), *Accountability in American education* (pp. 200–214). Boston: Allyn & Bacon.

Medsger, B. (1996). *Winds of change: Challenges confronting journalism education.* Arlington, VA: The Freedom Forum.

Morse, J. A., & Santiago, G., Jr. (2000). Accreditation and faculty. *Academe, 86*(1), 30–34.

National Commission on Excellence in Education. (1983). *A nation at risk: The imperative for educational reform.* Retrieved March 25, 2005, from http://www.ed.gov/pubs/ NatAtRisk/index.html

No Child Left Behind Act of 2001. (2002). Public law 107-110. January 8, 2002. Retrieved March 25, 2005, from http://www.ed.gov/policy/elsec/leg/esea02/index.html

Ohmann, R. (2000). Historical reflections on accountability. *Academe, X,* 24–29.

Planning for curricular change in journalism education. (1984). *The Oregon Report* (Project on the Future of Journalism and Mass Communication Education). Eugene: University of Oregon, School of Journalism.

Planning for curricular change in journalism education (2nd ed.). (1987). The Oregon Report. (Project of the Future of Journalism and Mass Communication Education). Eugene: University of Oregon, School of Journalism.

Rosenbaum, J. (1994). Assessment: An overview. In W. G. Christ (Ed.), *Assessing communication education: A handbook for media, speech, and theatre educators* (pp. 3–29). Hillsdale, NJ: Lawrence Erlbaum Associates, Inc.

Rowntree, D. (1992). *Exploring open and distance learning.* London: Kogan Page.

Sarlos, B. (1973). The complexity of the concept 'accountability' in the context of American education. In R. L. Leight (Ed.), *Philosophers speak on accountability in education* (pp. 65–81). Danville, IL: Interstate.

Strengthening the ties that bind: Integrating undergraduate liberal and professional study (Report of the Professional Preparation Network). (1988). Ann Arbor: The Regents of the University of Michigan.

Wagner, R. B. (1989). *Accountability in education: A philosophical inquiry.* New York: Routledge.

Wartella, E. (1994). Foreword. In *State of the field: Academic leaders in journalism, mass communication and speech communication look to the future at the University of Texas* (p. 1). Austin: The University of Texas at Austin, College of Communication.

2

Developing the Assessment Plan

Michael L. James
Harding University

R. Ferrell Ervin
Department of Communication
Southeast Missouri State University

The American university has changed dramatically since the establish-ment of the colleges in the 17th century. The colonial college's White male population is now religiously, ethnically, and racially diverse. The organizational structure has changed, the curriculum has been en-hanced, and the methods of academic delivery have been redefined (Pace, 1979, p. 133).

As the academic institutions have continually reinvented themselves, they have generally been treated with a "hands-off" attitude by most of their sponsors. Sometimes the goal of academic freedom clashed with "results" goals of elected officials. Regardless of the reason, public offi-cials generally only dealt with political issues like location of campuses and sizes of capital budgets (Zumeta, 2001, p. 155).

PUSH FOR ACCOUNTABILITY

Beginning in the 1980s, state governments announced intentions to carefully review the fiscal operation of the university and to require the university to intensify reporting of student academic achievement. This reaction was due to concerns that graduates were not readily employ-able after graduation. Recommendations included mission clarification, reemphasis on undergraduate instruction, rewarding of improved learn-ing, assessment of programs, and collection of data showing perform-ance (Ervin, 1988, pp. 19–23).

Because the institutions had used a "resource-and-reputation" model of excellence (Astin, 1985), quality depended on the quantity of campus resources, the quality of admitted students, and the reputation of faculty research. This model measured resource inputs but not the quality or quantity of outputs. Astin (1985) urged institutions to replace the model with a value-added concept that looked at the cognitive development of students from admission to graduation.

Some states initiated three performance-based initiatives to encourage or force improvement on the campuses: performance reporting, performance budgeting, and performance funding. Predictably, these mandates required publishing collective results, using results to determine budget allocations, and receiving rewards for achieving targeted results (Burke & Minassians, 2002, p. 15). Acceptable indicators usually fall into four types: inputs, processes, outputs, and outcomes.

Inputs include human, financial, and physical resources received to support programs. Processes involve the means used to deliver programs (i.e., methods of assessment, use of technology, teacher training). Outputs relate to the quantity of products produced (i.e., degrees awarded, retention or graduation rates, sponsored research funding). Outcomes are usually tied to the quality of the program, that is, test scores, job placements, satisfaction surveys, and alumni (Burke & Minassians, 2002, p. 36).

ENVIRONMENT FOR CHANGE

Although some successes were tied to these indicators, the call for greater scrutiny in higher education continued into the 1990s as financial pressures grew in states where corporations downsized because of expanding technology and globalization. As these corporations began to examine their practices, business leaders applied pressure on those associated with higher education to "streamline their production processes" just as the businesses had done. Business leaders stressed that the educational institutions should study customer satisfaction, examine quality control methods that were currently in place, and be able to prove the "outcomes" of their work. Birnbaum (2000) pointed out that although academics developed many management theories and considered them absolutely appropriate for business and government, those same academics believed that performance-based management clashed with academic culture (Birnbaum, 2000).

Accreditation bodies also saw the need for improved assessment. The Accrediting Council on Education in Journalism and Mass Communications (ACEJMC Accreditation, 2004) has adopted a new set of standards to require stiffer reviews starting in the 2005–2006 academic year.

CAMPUS RESISTANCE

Sarason (1998) has suggested that most in the academe did not readily embrace assessment requests. On the surface, assessment spread across the country, but most faculties considered assessment only an added burden and window dressing. Faculty chose to turn their collective backs, perhaps because of an aversion to the connotation of quantification and measurement (Ewell & Lisensky, 1988, p. 14), until most professional and regional accreditation agencies became involved.

Faculty also reject assessment because it could be viewed as interfering with autonomy and academic freedom (AAUP, 1995). These two conjoined, deep-seated professional beliefs suggest that worthwhile intellectual activity cannot survive in an atmosphere in which outside demands exercise a dominating influence over a professor's choice and action (Becher & Kogan, 1992, p. 101).

Another reason faculty avoid assessment is because they misunderstand its real purpose. Faculty may note that a typical student will complete 30 to 45 different courses, depending on the program. They point out that during the course of this undergraduate career, a student's performance would have been measured 30 to 45 separate times and by as many as 20 to 30 professors (Pace, 1979). Erroneously, they are looking at student achievement, not measurement of programs.

ENACTING A STRATEGY FOR MEASUREMENT

Graves (2002) suggested that as the impetus for assessment has grown, many institutions have reacted with a superficial approach, adopting quickly conceived approaches without thought of the individual character of the campus and have created assessment activities that don't produce meaningful data.

All planning should be centered on an understanding of the institution and its values and should strongly incorporate the faculty. Faculty satisfaction with institutional planning is a complex concept based on collegiality, workload, and autonomy (Pollicino, 1996). Participation, which has always been deemed as essential, is not always a sufficient condition for satisfaction with the results of the strategic planning process.

Sternberg and Grigorenko (2002) suggested that the theory of successful intelligence suggests that a student's failure to achieve at a level that matches his or her potential often is a direct result of teaching and assessment practices that are narrow in conceptualization and rigid in implementation. Ewell (1988) asserted that institutional assessment programs should be organized around (a) cognitive outcomes, (b) skills outcomes, (c) attitude and value outcomes, and (d) relationships.

Strategic planning, a planning model first developed in the corporate world and now widely used by universities, is based on a mission statement, goals, and objectives used to identify appropriate responses to internal and external conditions. Often viewed as a four-step program of research, goal setting, strategy determination, and evaluation, strategic planning is a deliberate model anchored by formative research of the environment in which the institution is located, environment within the organization, and the stakeholders of the institution. This research may be casual, secondary, or primary.

Casual research is information that is already known by stakeholders, persons who have experiences with the university (faculty, students, staff, administrators, alumni, citizens in the university's service region, and other helpful individuals).

Secondary research is information that is available from external or internal sources by turning to published reports, Internet listings, and previous self-studies that may have been prepared for regional and professional accrediting agencies.

Primary research is information that may not yet be publicly articulated by using a variety of research techniques like surveys and focus groups with the stakeholders.

The Institutional Mission Statement

Based on a careful examination of the findings obtained through the three described levels of research, an organization now has a grasp of the perceived history, development, and expectations that stakeholders hold. These are key elements concerning the impact of the university and they serve as a base on which to establish relevant goals and objectives. Those visionary goals may be broadly stated at the institutional level but become increasingly more specific as they are written for an institution's academic units. For example, the institution may list the following as a goal: (a) Offer a top-quality curriculum with a solid liberal education as a foundation for preparing graduates for leadership positions in society, or (b) provide a quality education that will lead to an understanding and philosophy of life consistent with Christian ideals.

Obviously, administrators will consider different approaches to prescribing their overall mission. Some will consider research a prime goal; others will include service to community or to religious beliefs. In all cases, administrators should involve elements of the faculty and staff at each decision step.

Expanded Statement of Institutional Purpose

Although the mission statement of the university is the foundation, it must be dissected, then expanded into several statements that incorporate the purpose of the university. These may include, but are not limited to, educational, social, physical, ethical, and cultural impact areas of the institution.

There is no definitive number of goals that should be written, and the goals will vary across the varied spectra of institutions. As an example of one set of goals, Harding University (2004, p. 5) developed six concise goal statements, each derived from the overall mission statement of the university. These statements include the following:

1. The integration of faith, learning, and living.
2. The development of Christian scholarship.
3. The promotion of Christian ethics.
4. The development of lasting relationships.
5. The promotion of wellness.
6. The promotion of citizenship within a global perspective.

Each of these statements is broadened with increasing definition, and each must be met by some working division or program within the institution (Table 2.1). An example of a fleshed-out "Expanded Statement of Institutional Purpose" (Nichols, 1995), coming from the goal statements, discussed earlier, might be as follows: "The University provides programs that enable students to acquire essential knowledge, skills, and dispositions in their academic disciplines for successful careers, advanced studies, and servant leadership" (p. 24).

Identification of Program Goals

Armed with the direction goals from the institution that have been expanded, the program directors and faculty choose the statement that will be assessed and derive plans for an acceptable match. In effect, the program goal will narrow the direction for assessment.

TABLE 2.1
Steps for Developing an Assessment Plan

Steps	Action	Example
1. Mission statement of institution	Administrators determine overall direction of institution	Provide a superb curriculum with an emphasis on core values that provides a foundation for preparing graduates for leadership positions in society
2. Expanded Statement of Institutional Purpose (ESIP)	Separate institutional mission into statements for each operation area	The university provides programs that enable students to acquire essential knowledge, skills, and dispositions in their academic areas for successful careers and advanced studies
3. Identify program goals	Identify working ESIP and refine program to match requisites	Students receiving a bachelor's degree in public relations will acquire the requisite academic tools needed to develop a successful career as a PR practitioner
4. Match goal statements to desired program outcomes	Prepare goals to determine if program is actually "doing" what it purports	Program graduates will be able to prepare a successful print and broadcast advertising campaign
5. Ascertain means of assessment and criteria for success	Develop direct and indirect measures that will allow a measure of outcomes of interest	In the Senior Seminar course, students will present a resume tape or disk media project. Eighty-five percent will be judged as Excellent or Superior (A or B) by the judgment of a three-member faculty panel
6. Collection of data	Use measurement tools to return quantitative and qualitative data	Based on results of a rubric from a three-member faculty panel, 90% of students were judged as excellent on a resume tape
7. Analysis and use of results	Use results of assessment to change or maintain program quality	As a result of low ratings on a public relations campaign assessment, the capstone course was revised to include new campaign components
8. Maintain a "culture" of assessment	Encourage faculty to value use of assessment	Faculty attitude changes from resistance to adoption; use of assessment is valued

The faculty for the program area should become involved with assessment at this stage. The faculty for each program area should see different niches for the preparation of individual goal statements. This goal statement will likely remain static for a long period. A goal statement for public relations might be as follows: "Students receiving a bachelor's degree in public relations will acquire the requisite academic tools needed to develop a successful career as a public relations practitioner."

The ACEJMC (ACEJMC Mission and Practices, 2004) suggested adopting a statement similar to the following for adoption by member schools:

> Professional programs should prepare students with a body of knowledge and a system of inquiry, scholarship and training for careers in which they are accountable to: the public interest for their knowledge, ethics, competence and service; citizens, clients or consumers for their competencies and the quality of their work; and employers for their performance. (p. 2)

Matching Goal Statements to Program Outcomes

This statement of goal mission becomes the "marching order" and the challenge for each academic unit. Each program must then decide on a strategy for reaching the goal. The educational unit now must choose several statements of intended outcomes that will be present if the institutional goal is to be met. These goals can and should be cognitive, behavioral, or attitudinal. Simply speaking, the outcome to be measured seeks to find out if we are "doing" what we purport to be doing. Are we fulfilling our goal? These intended educational outcomes are about our "product" (in this case, graduates of a program) and their ability to think (attitudes), know (cognitive), and do (behavioral). For example, the unit may list the following as one of its corresponding goals: "The School of Communication will provide a curriculum that encourages and enables students to think critically and creatively while incorporating the highest ethical and professional standards." Or, the unit might write the following: "Program graduates will feel confident about having problem-solving and industry software tools that will enable them to excel in all kinds of Web development environments." Or, it could write the following: "Program graduates will be able to prepare a professional public relations campaign."

Each of these statements of intended outcomes is appropriate for academic units, but they are very different in tone. The first requires a cognitive goal measurement, the second necessitates an attitudinal goal, and the third seeks a measurement of a behavioral goal.

Another academic unit wrote the following goals:

- Students will be able to recall important details in the brief history of the profession and to generalize about its future.
- Students will be able to relate the structures and practices of advertising to the functioning of agencies/corporations/not-for-profits.
- Students will be able to identify key legal aspects of the profession and relate significant causes to current professional practices.
- Students will be able to distinguish between various forms of syndicated audience data and primary research and derive information appropriate for an advertising campaign.

Of course, there are many intended outcomes for graduates of a successful program. The new ACEJMC standards (ACEJMC Mission and Practices, 2004, pp. 2–3) list 11 specific items desirable for a fully accredited program (see chapter 1).

Certainly not all of these ACEJMC competencies, or any other competencies, need to be evaluated in any single assessment cycle. Choices must be made to define areas that are essential to the unit, those where changes are expected, and ones that have shown concern as a result of unproven data or accusations. For example, if anecdotal data indicate that students are not prepared for the job market, an outcome that should be assessed might be employer satisfaction with graduates of the program.

How many statements of intended outcomes should be enacted? Three to five outcomes should be identified for each academic program (major) each year (Nichols & Nichols, 2000, p. 19). Obviously this is a starting point, and a few programs may require slightly more or less outcome statements.

For many reasons, the faculty should be the standard-bearer for writing these statements, not the program administrator. Concerns and fears of censorship of academic freedom will be alleviated if the faculty is at the helm of assessment goal statements. But more importantly, the faculty is closest to the content of an academic area and has a greater stake in the success and mission completion of the unit.

Although many possible statements for outcomes can be written, following are strategic choices that may be appropriate for consideration:

- The department will insure that all coursework is grounded in a historical, philosophical, legal, ethical, and cultural context.
- The department will establish a program for ongoing review of the existing curriculum.
- The department will establish a plan for ongoing review of other mass communication programs at benchmark institutions to determine trends in curricular design.

- The department will monitor changes in required competencies for entry-level positions in advertising, journalism, radio, public relations, and television, as well as current hiring trends.
- The department will establish and regularly seek input from a professional advisory panel about skills deemed necessary to function effectively in the increasingly technology-rich mass media professions.

These strategies were seen as clearly appropriate for an academic unit by one group of faculty members at their institution. However, they are not directly transferable to another institution without basing them on findings from the necessary casual, secondary, or primary research of the institutional stakeholders.

Because strategies can differ significantly, an assortment of methods or tactics must be developed for reaching those goals. After the faculty of an academic unit is satisfied with a proposed outcome that can be adequately measured, based on previously announced expectations, the academic organization evaluates or assesses the achievement of the stated objectives.

Means of Assessment and Criteria for Success

Planning the actual measurement of an outcome is integral with devising the intended outcome statements. If there is not a way to measure an outcome, obviously it should not be chosen. Among academe, hotly contested bitterness sometimes erupts when we try to ascertain results through "measurement" of students. Nichols and Nichols (2000) suggested that the difficulty arises because of a lack of clear understanding regarding the use of the term *measurable*, which faculty often consider defined as the following: (a) characterized by a microscope and six-decimal-place accuracy, (b) entirely quantified and precludes qualitative judgments, and (c) is perceived primarily as standardized cognitive examinations.

Nichols (1995) suggested that if the definition of "measurable" includes a general understanding of students' abilities to know, think, and do, agreement among faculty eases.

Statements of objectives should be quite prescriptive, and should answer affirmatively to the following questions suggested by Pratt (1995, p. 149):

1. Is the outcome consistent with the institution's Expanded Statement of Institutional Purpose?
2. Does the outcome describe a reasonable or achievable outcome?
3. Is the outcome clear and measurable?

4. Is the outcome written at a reasonable level of specificity?
5. Does the outcome specify the time frame in which it will be accomplished?

The National Laboratory for Higher Education (1974) indicated that an objective should be a single statement with the following parts:

1. Responsibility—What unit is responsible for performing the objective?
2. Outcome—What is expected to occur?
3. Time—When will the goal be completed?
4. Measurement—What tools will be used to measure the accomplishment of the objective?
5. Standards of Performance—What are the required attainment levels?
6. Conditions—What conditions must be met before the objectives can be accomplished?

An example of an objective to determine students' attitudes of their academic program is shown by the following proposed assessment:

On the senior exit survey for 2004–5 graduates, 80% of electronic media graduates will agree or strongly agree that they are prepared for entry-level positions in the field, and no more than 10% will disagree or strongly disagree.

In the Senior Seminar capstone electronic media course (Fall, 2004), students will present a resume tape or disk media project. 85% will be judged as Excellent or Superior (A or B) by the judgment of a five-member faculty panel.

Collection of Data

Although not covered in detail here, the measurements should be evaluated with the following points (Rogers, 1995, p. 165):

1. Content validity—Is there a correspondence between the test content and the departmental objectives?
2. Reliability—Are the scores consistent over time and across alternate forms?
3. Is the instrument appropriate for the target population?
4. Is the data normative to allow appropriate interpretation?

Analysis and Use of Results

All of the planning, scheduling, timing, and testing is worthless unless the final analysis is complete: How can these data be used to improve or assist the program? The end result is that a program is improved. The results should not be used to fix responsibility, especially for shortcomings, on an individual faculty member (Nichols & Nichols, 2000, p. 42). Assessment results, therefore, should not be used in personnel evaluation.

Rather, the end result should be program improvement. After the results of the assessment are tabulated, they should be spread across the faculty in the program and each member should become acquainted with them. Further, the results should indicate one of three courses of action, according to Nichols and Nichols (2000, p. 51):

1. The means of assessment should be changed and re-measured.
2. The findings may indicate that no changes should be made to the curriculum.
3. The assessment data should be used to change and improve the performance of the program and, therefore, the students.

Developing and Maintaining a "Culture" of Assessment

It sounds simple. The faculty knows what the academic organization is attempting. Each faculty member knows what material is going to be presented, what activities are considered to be most important, and how and why they and their colleagues will assess the accomplishment of the goal even before the plan begins. Faculty armed with a plan and students with a course syllabus have a target at which to aim. If it is so simple, then why do administrators and faculty frequently avoid implementing the strategic planning method? The answer frequently relates to the culture of the campus, the time required to formulate the plan, and the need to continually review and revise it.

This strategic planning process, rather than being static, is a method of continuous quality improvement. It goes beyond quality control or the desire to fix defects. It goes beyond quality assurance or the desire to design "high quality" into an academic program or a class in that program. It is an ongoing process to become "forever better" (Knight & Trowler, 2000). However, researchers caution that continuous quality improvement (CQI) is only possible when the ground rules include the following: (a) the idea that improvements can always be made, (b) the faculty is empowered to use their best judgment in creating the design, and (c) the faculty is committed to working with colleagues.

As can be predicted from the previous "prescription" for assessment success, a variety of techniques can be employed. An Internet search will provide many examples of methods that can be used, assuming the mission is the same.

The web master for the University of Nevada–Reno has compiled a "links page" that views assessment plans and examples of several institutions (Assessment Plan Examples, 2004). The connections reveal a variety of assessment plans for consideration.

Strategic planning and assessment help an institution or academic unit to focus its energy to systematically gather data useful in meeting a variety of campus and accrediting assessment demands. More importantly, strategic planning is a technique where faculty jointly set standards to be achieved in the presentation of course materials and standards of mastery for individual students.

When used as a continuous quality improvement tool, data gathered in the process can be formative or diagnostic to help faculty improve a program and enable the product, students, with better preparation to continue in their academic or professional careers.

REFERENCES

AAUP. (2005). *Academic freedom and tenure*. Retrieved August 9, 2005, from http://www.aaup.org/com-a/index.htm

ACEJMC Accrediting Standards. (2004). *ACEJMC Information Center*. Retrieved from http://www.ukans.edu/~acejmc/PROGRAM/STANDARDS.SHTML

ACEJMC Mission and Practices. (2004). *ACEJMC Information Center*. Retrieved from http://www.ukans.edu/~acejmc/BREAKING/newprins.shtml

Assessment Plan Examples. (2004). Retrieved from http://www.unr.edu/assess/PlanResources/ResourcesPages/OtherInstitutionLinks.asp

Astin, A. (1985). *Achieving academic excellence*. San Francisco: Jossey-Bass.

Becher, T., & Kogan, M. (1992). *Process and structure in higher education* (2nd ed.). New York: Routledge.

Birnbaum, R. (2000). *Management fads in higher education: Where they come from, what they do, why they fail*. San Francisco: Jossey-Bass.

Burke, J., & Minassians, H. (2002). *Reporting higher education results: Missing links in the performance chain*. San Francisco: Jossey-Bass.

Ervin, R. (1988). Outcomes assessment: The rationale and the implementation. In R. L. Hoskins (Ed.), *Insights* (pp. 19–23). Columbia, SC: ASJMC.

Ewell, P. (1984). *The self-regarding institution: Information for excellence*. Boulder, CO: NCHEMS.

Ewell, P., & Lisensky, R. (1988). *Assessing institutional effectiveness: Redirecting the self-study process*. Boulder, CO: The Consortium for the Advancement of Private Higher Education.

Graves, D. (2002). *Testing is not teaching: What should count in education*. Portsmouth, NH: Heinemann.

Harding University Catalog. (2004). *General Catalog*. Searcy, AR: The Harding Press.

Knight, P. T., & Trowler, P. R. (2000). Academic work and quality. *Quality in Higher Education, 6*(2), 109–114.

National Laboratory for Higher Education. (1974). *Developing measurable objectives*. Durham, NC: Author.

Nichols, J. (1995). *A practitioner's handbook for institutional effectiveness and student outcomes assessment implementation*. New York: Agathon Press.

Nichols, J., & Nichols, K. (2000). *The departmental guide and record book for student outcomes assessment and institutional effectiveness* (3rd ed.). New York: Agathon Press.

Pace, C. (1979). *Measuring outcomes of college: Fifty years of findings and recommendations for the future*. San Francisco: Jossey-Bass.

Pollicino, E. B. (1996). *Faculty satisfaction with institutional support as a complex concept: Collegiality, workload, autonomy*. Paper presented at the annual meeting of the American Educational Research Association, New York.

Pratt, L. (1995). Statements of outcomes/objectives and assessment at the department level. In J. Nichols (Ed.), *A practitioner's handbook for institutional effectiveness and student outcomes assessment implementation* (pp. 146–156). New York: Agathon Press.

Rogers, B. (1995). Setting and evaluating intended educational (instructional) outcomes. In J. Nichols (Ed.), *A practitioner's handbook for institutional effectiveness and student outcomes assessment implementation* (pp. 157–171). New York: Agathon Press.

Sarason, S. B. (1998). *Political leadership and educational failure*. San Francisco: Jossey-Bass.

Sternberg, R., & Grigorenko, E. (2002). The theory of successful intelligence as a basis for instruction and assessment in higher education. In D. Halapren (Ed.), *Applying the science of learning to university teaching and beyond* (pp. 45–53). San Francisco: Jossey-Bass.

Zumeta, W. (2001). Public policy and accountability in higher education: Lessons from the past and present for the new millennium. In D. E. Heller (Ed.), *The states and public higher education policy: Affordability, access, and accountability*. Baltimore: The Johns Hopkins University Press.

Mission Statements[1]

William G. Christ
Department of Communication
Trinity University

Terry Hynes
College of Journalism and Communications
University of Florida

All media education programs have missions. Some missions are explicit, visionary, and useful; some are implicit, unclear, and fractured. Mission statements are "political" documents that can be used to clarify or obfuscate a unit's reality (Christ & Blanchard, 1994). They can accurately mirror a vision or simply reflect a pipe dream.

Departments might argue that they have implicit mission statements or that no matter what the mission statement says it is the faculty, courses, and facilities that define a program. Although there is merit in this argument, Blanchard and Christ (1993) argued that "explicit mission statements should be at the center of curricular discussion" (p. 82).

In a 1990 survey distributed to 258 member schools of the Broadcast Education Association, less than 56% of the large schools' departments and less than 50% of the medium and small schools' departments were identified as having mission statements (Warner & Liu, 1990). Given the growing adoption of strategic planning processes by universities in the 1980s, this was a surprisingly small number. For those seeking accreditation from the Accrediting Council on Education in Journalism and Mass Communications (ACEJMC), mission statements are an expected part of the accreditation process.

---

[1]Some of the arguments and earlier versions of this chapter can be found in Blanchard and Christ (1993), Christ and Blanchard (1994), and Christ and Hynes (1997).

In the mid-1990s, two task forces of the Association for Education in Journalism and Mass Communication (AEJMC) attempted to develop mission statements for the field. The AEJMC Vision 2000 Task Force (AEJMC, 1994a, 1994b) articulated the mission for Journalism and Mass Communication (JMC) education when it wrote:

> Since we are all consumers and to some extent producers, communication skills—in terms of both producing and interpreting messages—should be part of the basic education in a democratic society. The goal of journalism and mass communication programs is to provide students *and* the larger society with a deeper understanding of mass communication processes and to improve the practices and performance of mass media professionals. Their goal is to produce socially responsible, informed, skilled citizens who understand how various media technologies and communication processes emerge within particular social, economic, and political contexts, and thereby affect both individual identity and societal processes on a global level. Journalism and mass communication have become vital to the maintenance of an informed society. Knowledge of how we speak, how we write and think, how we inform, interpret and persuade—as well as how we are spoken to, how we are addressed, how we are envisioned, informed and persuaded—are now critical for educated people. (p. 6, italics in the original)

In 1995, after a review of numerous studies of journalism and mass communication education completed between 1982 and 1995, the AEJMC Curriculum Task Force concluded "The purpose of media education is to produce well-rounded graduates who have critical thinking skills as well as practical skills, and who have an understanding of the philosophy of the media and a dedication to the public service role that the media have in our society" (AEJMC, 1996, p. 106).

Mission statements are required for those wishing to be ACEJMC accredited. Standard 1, "Mission, Governance and Administration," of the AECJMC accreditation guidelines states that, "The policies and practices of the unit ensure that it has an effectively and fairly administered working and learning environment" (ACEJMC, 2004, p. 42). The first of the five required indicators for this standard focuses precisely on the importance of the mission statement: "The unit has a mission statement and engages in strategic or long-range planning that provides vision and direction for its future, identifies needs and resources for its mission and goals and is supported by university administration outside the unit" (ACEJMC, 2004, p. 42).

As part of its "Principles of Accreditation," ACEJMC states the mission of journalism and mass communications education as:

> Professional programs should prepare students with a body of knowledge and a system of inquiry, scholarship and training for careers in which they

are accountable to: the public interest for their knowledge, ethics, competence and service; citizens, clients or consumers for their competencies and the quality of their work; and employers for their performance. (ACEJMC, 2004, p. 13)

It presents the mission of the profession: "The mission of journalism and mass communications professions in a democratic society is to inform, to enlighten and to champion freedoms of speech and press. These professions seek to enable people to fulfill their responsibilities as citizens who mean to govern themselves" (ACEJMC, 2004, p. 13).

Apparently, there are still schools that do not think explicit mission statements are needed. Although trying to articulate mission statements is not easy, especially if there are disparate positions that are held by the tenured faculty, the debate that ensues when trying to develop statements can be very useful and important. If a program does not have a mission statement, the faculty can be asked to look at themselves, the facilities, and the courses and curricula and ask the following questions: What would an external review group say was the mission of this media program? What is it doing? Although coming across as a hypothetical exercise, in reality, the answer to the question, "What is your mission?" is very important to deans, vice presidents of academic affairs, and presidents. Programs need to be able to justify their existence to a wide range of people or else risk losing the support of administrators or legislatures. As Galvin (1992, p. 24) suggested, developing goals and mission statements can produce at least four benefits: (a) clarifying organizational purpose, (b) forcing consensus on what is important, (c) creating a framework against which to evaluate resource allocation, and (d) reinforcing a commitment to student learning.

WHAT SHOULD MISSION STATEMENTS LOOK LIKE?

Although there is not a cookbook answer to the question, "What should mission statements look like?" there have been recommendations about what a mission statement could contain. For example, Ackoff (1986), in a book dealing with writing mission statements for businesses, wrote that a mission statement should have five characteristics. First, "*it should contain a formulation of the firm's objectives that enables progress toward them to be measured.* To state objectives that cannot be used to evaluate performance is hypocrisy" (p. 39, italics in original). It is important that the objectives of a mission statement are not simply a string of "operationally meaningless superlatives such as *biggest, best, optimum, and maximum*" (Ackoff, 1986, p. 38, italics in original). This first characteristic is especially important in an age of accountability. Viable assessment strategies need to tap not only what is taught but what is learned. Mission statements and objectives should be linked so that measurable assessment strategies can be developed.

Ackoff's (1986) second characteristic is that "*a company's mission statement should differentiate it from other companies.* It should establish the individuality, if not the uniqueness of the firm" (p. 39, italics in original). The question for media programs is as follows: What is the unique, intellectual, academic contribution of the media program to the university? Programs that are too similar to other programs within the same university may open themselves up to being merged or eliminated.

Ackoff's (1986) third point is "*a mission statement should define the business that the company wants to be in, not necessarily is in*" (p. 40, italics in original). From technical schools to liberal arts and sciences colleges to research universities, from teaching programs to research institutes, the "business" of education is diverse. This point underscores that mission statements should be powerful statements of vision. "Not only should they clarify a unit's objectives and distinctiveness, but they should illuminate a unit's potential" (Blanchard & Christ, 1993, p. 83).

Ackoff's (1986) fourth suggestion is that "*a mission statement should be relevant to all the firm's stakeholders. . . .* The mission should state how the company intends to serve each of them" (p. 41, italics in original). Programs in higher education serve a number of stakeholders including students, alumni, faculty, staff, administrators, parents, legislators, and so forth. A mistake a unit can make is to "forget" that one of its largest stakeholders is the university or college as a whole. Linking the unit's mission statement to the university's mission statement is critical. If a unit does not firmly position its mission within the mission of the university as a whole, it becomes easier for administrators to see the unit as a "loose cannon" that needs to be controlled.

The last characteristic of a mission statement, according to Ackoff (1986), is that "*a mission statement should be exciting and inspiring.* It should motivate all those whose participation in its pursuit is sought. . . . It does *not* have to appear to be feasible; it only has to be *desirable . . .*" (p. 41, italics in original). In the current era of accountability, Ackoff's comment that a mission does not have to appear to be feasible may not serve a unit well. Outcomes should be linked to mission statements, and therefore, the mission statements need to be in a language that is exciting, inspiring, and feasible.

To Ackoff's (1986) list should be added the following: "The mission statement should accurately reflect the educational philosophy of your program" and "should reflect the mission statement of the university/ college in which the unit is housed" (Blanchard & Christ, 1993, p. 84).

Combining these characteristics, we might come up with a list of questions that include: Who are we? What needs do we address and how do we analyze or respond to those needs? How do we respond to key constituents? What is our philosophy or core values? What makes us unique or distinctive? How do we know when we are true to our mission or when we veer off course? How do we create ways to readdress systematically our mission and goals? (Blanchard & Christ, 1993, adapted from Bryson, 1988, p. 105; Galvin, 1992, p. 23; see also Appendix A for another series of questions about mission statements).

STATEMENTS OF MISSION AND PURPOSE

Although media education programs have much in common, they also differ, based variously on the nature of the missions of their institutions (e.g., whether teaching or research is the main focus), university or program size, university or program service areas (e.g., local–regional focus or national–international focus), disciplines included within the media unit or the disciplinary unit in which a media program is housed (e.g., a media program which includes traditional speech and rhetoric-based curricula or media instruction housed in an English Department), and structural program configuration (e.g., a department within a larger college or an independent media college or department). Any combination of these factors can lead to different visions and missions for a media unit. Thus, it is clear that there is no one mission for media education but rather a variety of missions and purposes. (The following examples are from a Christ & Hynes (1997) Association for Education in Journalism and Mass Communication/Association of Schools of Journalism and Mass Communication Education Joint Committee report. The names of the schools have been removed because the quotes are meant to be illustrative of the ideas presented and may no longer apply to the specific programs.)

With respect to Ackoff's (1986) first characteristic, linking measurable objectives to mission statements can be used to indicate success. Whether it is ACEJMC, state, or regional accreditation, assessment has become an important part of what we are expected to do as educators. Programs need to be prepared to use their mission statements and objectives as a focal point of their assessment strategies (Christ, 1994, 1995, 1997). For example, one school stated that its mission was "to educate, train and develop students to become professional journalists, broadcasters, graphic artists/photographers, advertising and public relations practitioners and to serve as liberally educated members of the institutions, communities and societies in which they live and work"

(Christ & Hynes, 1997, p. 78). It then listed six "intended outcomes" linked to the mission: graduating people who were

> good writers and communicators; knowledgeable of the necessary equipment and technologies in journalism and communications; practically trained through internships, production work, professionally affiliated clubs, projects and related activities; skilled to enter, maintain and advance in their chosen media or related professional careers and goals; counseled by teachers, program advisers and others to understand the role and impact of the media and practitioners; creative, adaptable and aware of the ever-changing needs of the multimedia professions and the interdependent world in which they live, work and make their contributions. (Christ & Hynes, 1997, p. 79)

The point is that these objectives, which were linked to the mission statement, provide a framework which can ultimately, after each objective is carefully "operationalized," be used to measure success (see Appendix B).

Ackoff's (1986) second characteristic encourages mission statements that identify a program's uniqueness relative to other programs. This can be approached from at least two directions. First, a media program obtains an advantage (especially in a time of reduced or limited resources) by indicating what unique or special contributions it makes to the university as a whole. The program may be similar to other programs at other universities, but it should not be similar to other programs in the same university. Second, to the extent that media programs in different universities identify similar ways in which they uniquely contribute to their institutions, the constellation of those "similarly unique" elements may be identified as a basis of shared roles for media programs across institutions.

The uniqueness of different programs tends to fall into three categories: specialized knowledge, values, skills, and objectives of the program; the special publics or stakeholders with which they are concerned; and a particular environment of which they are part or are trying to create. (These similarly unique characteristics are also discussed later, in the "Patterns" section.)

Knowledge, Values, Skills, and Objectives

Some schools emphasize their uniqueness in terms of knowledge, values, skills, or objectives. For example, a school might choose to accentuate the technology and the global aspects of its orientation by stating the following:

"The department embraces technology as a communication tool, celebrates its commitment to professionalism, and leads the campus community in the use of technology, globalization initiatives, and diversity by reaching out to other units on campus, other universities, both internationally and domestically, and to the communication industry in collaborative curricular, teaching, research, and creative opportunities." (p. 79)

Others tend to be very specific about different kinds of courses or areas of study when they indicate that they want to "introduce students to the historical, public policy, legal, and ethical issues related to the roles and effects of the mass media as important social institutions" (p. 79).

Still other programs stress an integration of particular areas, whether it be scholarly work and professional practice or "through a program that is both integrative and holistic—one which introduces students to the intellectual traditions and disciplines, to the rest of higher education, and to contemporary communications practice" (p. 79).

Some programs might list a variety of skills students are required to master, including critical thinking, information gathering, and written, oral, and visual communication skills, reporting, and production. The uniqueness of programs often is reflected in the clustering of these skills, or in the way in which the skills are associated with other elements deemed valuable in the program. For example, schools have argued that graduates of their schools "should be well grounded in the liberal arts and instilled with the skills to make critical inquiry into matters of culture, technology, ethics, and responsibilities of the media in the world," whereas others stress "critical thinking, creativity, and personal integrity, or the development of basic skills in writing, mathematics, foreign language, and computers" (p. 80).

Some programs stress professional or personal values when they include statements like the following in their missions: "to imbue students with the highest ethical and professional standards so that they understand and address competently the diversity of issues and ideas that confront them now and in the 21st century" (p. 80). Others demonstrate how values and knowledge are intertwined:

"The ability of people to govern themselves in a democratic society can be no better than the quality of news and information they receive. The Founding Fathers recognized this principle in the First Amendment, which attempts to guarantee that no government can censor the free flow of information, information which people need in order to be informed and to think critically and well. This principle is just as vital in our modern world, where the lack of timely, reliable, high-quality information leads to erroneous impressions and flawed public policy. . . . (Our program) prepares students to search for, gather, and present news in words and pictures according to the highest standards of truth, honesty, fairness, clarity, courage, independence, importance, perseverance, and service to the democratic ideals that underlie the First Amendment." (p. 80)

Programs in colleges affiliated with or sponsored by a particular religion, might include a spiritual dimension in their mission statements: "The mission . . . is to plan, organize, and implement an undergraduate and graduate journalism and mass communication teaching program that reflects commitment to the education of an effective graduate who will appreciate the interaction of spiritual, academic, societal, and professional values within the context of the university and college missions" (p. 80).

Still other programs stress their own values or commitments over student values when they write that they are "committed to free speech, freedom of the press, and open inquiry" (p. 81).

Specific Outcomes. Although some mission statements emphasize courses or areas of study, skills, and values as intrinsic components of the program, other mission statements might frame their role in terms of *outcomes*: we want to graduate students who "recognize the value of thorough reporting and understand the public has a right to accurate information reported fairly" (p. 81). Or, graduates of the undergraduate program are expected to understand the "(a) roles, structures, and functions of a free American press within a global society; (b) the roles and functions of advertising and public information within society; and (c) a professional communicator's roles, functions, process, and skills of the specialty area within the profession" (p. 81).

Whom the Faculty Were Trying to Serve

Higher education serves a variety of "publics" or stakeholders. Whether it is the students, practitioners, or the community at large, many mission statements show their uniqueness by emphasizing whom they want to attract or serve. As one might expect from professionally oriented media programs, the industries and professional practices for which programs prepare students are key stakeholders reflected in many media statements. This is most evident in the mission statement and standards developed by ACEJMC for accreditation (presented earlier in this chapter).

Christ and Hynes (1997) found that of the 176 mission and purpose statements they analyzed, 121 (68.7%) indicated that part of their mission was to prepare students for specific industries (e.g., newspapers, broadcasting, public relations, advertising) or to provide students with specific professional skills that could be used in such industries (e.g., reporting, graphics design, advertising strategies). Forty (22.7%) explicitly noted a commitment either to attract or serve a diverse faculty or student population, or, in some other way, to foster racial or cultural diversity. Language consistent with this commitment included the following: (a) "to attract and nurture a diverse student body and faculty providing students with attitudes in harmony with America's pluralistic society and consistent with the liberal education philosophies of higher education," or (b) "the school contributes to and uses state-of-the-art knowledge in the fields of print and broadcast journalism; radio, television and film; human and mass communication; communication sciences and disorders, and advertising and public relations, with particular emphases on unserved, underserved and under-represented populations" (Christ & Hynes, 1997, pp. 81–82).

Service to practitioners and the community also is talked about in the "Patterns" section later.

Unique Environment in Which the Program Is Located or Environment the Program Is Trying to Create

Some programs cite location as a special part of their mission, either because they are state-supported institutions or because they see their environment as an important educational element of what they offer. Some programs focus on the advantages, opportunities, and special commitments of their geographic location in articulating their mission, saying things like, "This setting allows students to combine academic and professional interests in a program that matches precept with example, education with experience. The setting also allows the faculty to be responsive to the needs of the communication industry and area professionals through programs of research, continuing education, and professional service" (p. 82).

Other programs describe their mission, in part, as creating a special "place" or "environment." An example is a program that said its department and faculty

"strive to provide an educational environment wherein students analyze the theories and concepts of communication, consider its history and impact, and develop a level of expertise in production and performance. The department ensures students the opportunity and educational foundation to consider societal implications and ethical considerations of communication practices, procedures and policies." (p. 82)

As noted earlier in this chapter, Ackoff's (1986) third characteristic of mission statements concerns the power of the vision they reflect or their potential to move a program to a new level of its growth and development. Some programs use the word *vision* in statements that precede their mission statements. Others incorporate a more comprehensive vision into their statements of purpose. The ACEJMC vision statement, for example, includes the following:

> Journalism and mass communication transmit and interpret culture and bind society together, making them among the most vital forces in the maintenance of any society and fundamental to democratic government and a free society. They embody the spirit of a free press and are central to the preservation and advancement of the values provided under the First Amendment.
>
> Because of their importance to society, journalism and mass communication demand the highest possible level of integrity, fairness, understanding, and skill from both practitioners of journalism and mass communications and the educators who teach the practitioners. (ACEJMC, 2004, p. 8)

A "vision" of the role and function of media programs within the broader communications field and within the traditions of the liberal arts is also stated by some:

> "The school is part of the rapidly changing field of communication, and journalism and mass communication (JMC) is an essential, founding component of that field. It is a tradition of teaching and inquiry that sees professional media education as a discourse deeply embedded in the spirit and substance of the liberal arts, modern and ancient. The skills taught in the JMC curriculum—information-gathering, writing, editing, message creation, oral presentation, interpretation, criticism and the harnessing of technology to human needs—are fundamental tools of liberal education in every age." (p. 83)

For some programs, the environment they are trying to create includes not only preparing people for careers but also elevating, improving, or challenging the current practice of the profession: "The faculty is committed to a scholarly environment in which theoretical, historical, critical, and technological methodologies help students to question, challenge, and improve all forms of communication" (p. 83).

Mission statements which are relevant to all of an organization's stakeholders is Ackoff's (1986) fourth characteristic, as noted earlier. The following illustrates how this characteristic can be included in a unit's mission statement: "In broad terms, the department's primary objective is to help students acquire knowledge, understanding and skills. . . . The department, however, also seeks to serve the university and its objectives, and to provide service to high schools and community colleges in the state, to local news media and professional associations, to its own alumni, and to the community in general" (p. 83).

Some programs state their linkages to the larger university: "The principal mission of the Communication Department derives from those of the university and the College of Arts and Sciences in which the department is housed: to provide a firm grounding in the liberal arts and sciences and strong professional preparation, to the end that students are educated for satisfying lives and successful careers" (p. 84).

As indicated earlier, mission statements should reflect the educational philosophies of their programs. However, mission and purpose statements alone are not adequate evidence on which to judge the entire educational philosophy of a program. Shades of differences between programs with similar missions also may not be clear from mission statements alone.

PATTERNS

As noted earlier, there are similarities among different media programs and their mission statements. Analyzing those similarities can lead to a deeper understanding of the core values and other elements that help create a unified field of study in journalism and mass communication.

Professional Education and the Liberal Arts

One of the most fundamental questions addressed by media education mission and purpose statements concerns the relation of the programs to the liberal arts and sciences. If one end of a continuum of media education is a trade school orientation that stresses skills to the exclusion of contextual courses like history, economics, philosophy, psychology, English, or mass media processes and effects, the other end of the continuum is an orientation that stresses studies courses to the exclusion of application to practice.

Many programs embrace the idea that media education involves preparing a liberally educated professional. Even programs which express a near-balance in combining professional preparation with a liberal arts context, however, differ in some of the nuances of that balance.

Mission Statement Language. Examples of broad mission statement language include the following: (a) to "prepare students for productive and socially responsible careers in journalism and mass communication in the context of a liberal education"; (b) to "educate students broadly in the liberal arts, enabling them to become productive and creative citizens and leaders in their profession, community, and nation"; (c) "to develop liberally educated, professionally trained communicators who are equipped intellectually and ethically to convey the issues of contemporary society" (p. 85); and (d) to provide "educational experiences that enrich and integrate the liberal arts and sciences with communication and media studies and practices. To this end, the Department of Communication seeks to educate students (a) to become communicators and media sense-makers, for themselves, their clients, and their communities; (b) to understand their obligations as citizens within global and cultural communication contexts shaped by media; and (c) to recognize their opportunities and responsibilities as ethical, self-directed .practitioners within changing information, technological, and communication environments" (p. 85).

Specific Mission Statement Language. Examples of more specific mission statement language linked to specific media education areas include the following: (a) "The Communication Department strives to provide quality education to students to enable them to speak, write, and think clearly, critically, and creatively. The department is committed to a liberal education in the arts and sciences as well as to professional training in the skills of journalism, public relations, advertising, video technology, and speech communication"; (b) "to provide professional education in the areas of advertising, journalism (print and broadcast), and public relations, in the context of a strong college liberal arts curriculum . . ."; and (c) "to prepare students for careers in journalism and public relations by teaching professional skills and media research techniques; to increase the importance of a broad liberal arts basis of education so that students are educated 'for life,' not just for a living; to retain the traditional, basic strengths of a media-based curriculum—information gathering, writing, editing, media law, and ethics, while adapting the curriculum to dramatic changes in mass communication professionals" (pp. 85–86).

Teaching, Research, and Service

Another framing device for articulating a program's mission or purpose lies in the three traditional university mission areas of teaching, research (and creative activities), and service. Many schools expect faculty to teach, conduct research, and serve their schools, communities, and profession. Some schools include this expectation in their mission statements when they state that their school "recognizes three important parts to its academic and professional mission—to educate undergraduate and graduate students, to create and disseminate knowledge, and to provide service that will enhance standards of performance"; or that the college "focuses its activities on instruction in the professional disciplines of journalism and mass communications; adding to the body of knowledge in those professions through research, scholarship, and creative activity; and service to those professions and to the community at large." Other media programs stress one of the three areas (teaching, research, or service): "Teaching is the single most important responsibility of a . . . faculty member" (p. 86).

Practitioner, Citizen, and Consumer Preparation

Preparation to Be a Practitioner. Although most media programs explicitly see their mission as preparing people for careers, the discussion of career preparation differs in terms of how and where it is emphasized in mission statements. Some mission statements say that career preparation is the primary mission: (a) "The primary goal of the Division of Mass Communication is to train students to be effective and productive communicators using mass media as a tool"; or (b) "our mission is to provide students the concepts and skills necessary to enter mass communication careers in a socially responsible way, and the resources to think critically about the role and impact of mass communication in society" (p. 87).

Some mission statements suggest that preparation is part of a broader mission or context and are specific about how career preparation requires knowledge (understanding), skills, and value: the mission "is to advance the profession of journalism by educating highly skilled and broadly knowledgeable professionals with a passion for their craft.

This is accomplished in two ways. First, the faculty must encourage an understanding of the role of mass media in the contemporary socio-cultural, political, and economic environment, and an appreciation for journalistic principles and traditions. Second, the faculty must teach the skills for gathering, analyzing, and communicating information effectively" (p. 87).

Teaching communication skills is mentioned in a number of mission statements: (a) the mission is "to develop effective communication skills among our students . . . to prepare students for careers in advertising, broadcasting, journalism, and public relations . . ."; or (b) "our goal is to instill the fundamental skills necessary for a journalist—writing, reporting, and interviewing" (p. 87).

Critical or analytical thinking is another explicit theme mentioned across mission statements: the mission of our program (a) "is to teach its students to think critically and to apply that thinking to the collection, organization, and communication of information through the public media. Analytical thinking is essential to clear writing, which is at the heart of good journalism"; (b) "we teach students to gather information, to present it clearly and to think critically within a legal and ethical framework"; or (c) one of our instructional goals is "to provide intellectual preparation that emphasizes the capacity to think critically and creatively, the ability to solve problems effectively in a professional context, and the ability to cope with change in the professional world . . ." (pp. 87–88).

Some mission statements attempt to place the teaching of skills within a broad context: the department's goal "is to develop liberally educated women and men who understand the vital role of the written and spoken symbol as they adapt to and challenge their environments, and who can express themselves accurately, clearly, grammatically, creatively, and persuasively . . . while we teach our students specific skills required to perform effectively in the communications-related industries and arts, those same skills—writing, reporting, speaking, listening, thinking creatively—are broadly applicable to a wide range of careers and interests. Mastery of them assures a student a life of flexibility and enrichment, no matter what career paths and changes he or she might choose" (p. 88).

Preparation to Be a Citizen or Consumer. Some programs explicitly state that their mission is to educate students as citizens and consumers: (a) "To educate undergraduate students so they are productive citizens in the communities in which they live . . ."; (b) "to educate consumers about the functions and importance of news media and related agencies in American life"; or (c) "to foster informed citizens and consumers of the media by offering course work for general education" (p. 88).

The Nonmajor Student

Being committed to the liberal arts for many programs means making sure that students get a liberal education from outside the unit while professional education and training is provided inside the unit. However, some programs see their mission as being to serve the liberal education needs of nonmajors and the general student, a position which programs sometimes use to argue their centrality to the total university mission: a program can argue that its mission is to (a) "contribute to the enhancement of liberal arts education in the university"; (b) "students from other disciplines, seeking to improve their communications skills and knowledge about the media and their impact on society, will find a variety of course offerings"; (c) the program "articulates the connection between communication and the purpose of the university . . . communication is central to the mission of the university"; or (d) the aim is "to provide all students with the opportunity to gain an understanding of the principles, processes, and practices of human communication through a series of foundational courses. These courses are designed to assist in the preparation for careers in law, teaching, business, and other related fields" (p. 88).

Linkage to Practitioners and the Community

Some programs specify in their mission statements their relationship to practitioners and the general community. This aspect of mission statements differs from the earlier discussion regarding programs' role in preparing a student to be a practitioner, citizen, or consumer. Rather, this aspect of the mission statements articulates linkages to practitioners or the community.

Linkage to Practitioners. In terms of practitioners, the relationship is presented in three ways. First, practitioners are seen as a resource for schools. Second, schools see themselves as offering educational opportunities to practitioners. Third, schools see the program–practitioner relationship as mutually beneficial. An example of the first is a school which states that it includes national leaders from the communications industry on an advisory board explicitly to support the unit's mission. An example of the second is a school that offers continuing education to regional professionals. The third is exemplified in statements such as the following: "Faculty members work to maintain mutually constructive relationships with professional and academic communities by sharing expertise and knowledge with appropriate local, national, and international organizations" (p. 89).

Linkages to the Community.   Linkages to the community also tend to fall into three categories. First, are programs that create linkages when they refer to their students as part of the larger community: "founded on the premise that college students will graduate into a changing world. Success in that world is contingent on their ability to adapt by calling on appropriate knowledge, skills, and abilities when needed" (p. 89).

The second category suggests that the educational unit should serve the community through such things as continuing education: the school "has a major role to play in providing short-term educational opportunities to regional, national, and international communities with nondegree programs offered through corporate, nonprofit, and governmental agencies" (p. 89).

The third category of statements link media programs to the community by including statements about the important social purposes of media and the programs' function to educate students about the role of media in society: a program "provides students with a dynamic program of skills and conceptual courses devoted to the practice and social impact of journalism" (p. 89).

SUMMARY

Media education mission statements and statements of purpose are as diverse as the programs, colleges, and universities they represent. Even when many programs include the same value or components, the context of programs and the discussion may radically alter the salience of that value or component from one program to another. Even so, there are patterns or commonalities across many programs.

Though it is hard work and can take many hours of intense negotiations among faculty, developing a mission statement is an important step in the assessment process. If taken seriously, the mission statement can be a touchstone for faculty as they grapple with the difficult intellectual work of developing student learning outcomes and measurements.

REFERENCES

Accrediting Council on Education in Journalism and Mass Communication. (2004). *Journalism and mass communications accreditation, 2004–2005.* Lawrence, KS: Author.

Ackoff, R. L. (1986). *Management in small doses.* New York: Wiley.

Association for Education in Journalism and Mass Communication Curriculum Task Force. (1996). Responding to the challenge of change. *Journalism and Mass Communication Educator, 50*(4), 101–119.

Association for Education in Journalism and Mass Communication Vision 2000 Task Force. (1994a, August). *Report No. 1: The identity and structure of the AEJMC.* Report presented at the annual convention of the AEJMC, Atlanta, GA.

Association for Education in Journalism and Mass Communication Vision 2000 Task Force. (1994b, August). *Report No. 2: The viability of JMC units within universities.* Report presented at the annual convention of the AEJMC, Atlanta, GA.

Blanchard, R. O., & Christ, W. G. (1993). *Media education and the liberal arts: A blueprint for the new professionalism.* Hillsdale, NJ: Lawrence Erlbaum Associates, Inc.

Bryson, J. M. (1988). *Strategic planning for public and nonprofit organizations.* San Francisco: Jossey-Bass.

Christ, W. G. (Ed.). (1994). *Assessing communication education: A handbook for media, speech, and theatre educators.* Hillsdale, NJ: Lawrence Erlbaum Associates, Inc.

Christ, W..G. (1995). The role of journalism and mass communication education in the university of the future. Speech given during the 1993 AEJMC plenary session. *Insights* (Winter). Columbia, SC: Association of Schools of Journalism and Mass Communication.

Christ, W. G. (Ed.). (1997). *Media education assessment handbook.* Mahwah, NJ: Lawrence Erlbaum Associates, Inc.

Christ, W. G., & Blanchard, R. O. (1994). Mission statements, outcomes and the new liberal arts. In W. G. Christ (Ed.), *Assessing communication education* (pp. 31–55). Hillsdale, NJ: Lawrence Erlbaum Associates, Inc.

Christ, W. G., & Hynes, T. (1997). The missions and purposes of journalism and mass communication education. *Journalism and Mass Communication Educator, 52*, 74–98.

Erwin, P. T. (1991). *Assessing student learning and development.* San Francisco: Jossey-Bass.

Galvin, K. N. (1992). Foundation for assessment: The mission, goals and objectives. In E. A. Hay (Ed.), *Program assessment in speech communication* (pp. 21–24). Annandale, VA: Speech Communication Association.

Warner, C., & Liu, Y. (1990). Broadcast curriculum profile (a freeze-frame look at what BEA members offer students). *Feedback, 31*(3), 6–7.

Whitney, D. R. (1970). Improving essay examinations: I. Writing, essay questions. *Technical Bulletin No. 9.* Iowa City: Evaluation and Examination Service, University of Iowa.

APPENDIX A: QUESTIONS ABOUT MISSION STATEMENTS (FROM CHRIST & BLANCHARD, 1994, PP. 49–50)

1. Does our program have an explicit mission statement?

2. When was the last time we discussed our mission and/or mission statement?

3. How well does the mission of our academic program reflect and support the mission of our institution as a whole?

4. If an outside group came to our school, what would it identify as our strengths and weaknesses?

5. How committed are we to the general education of non-majors? What kinds of experiences (e.g., courses, apprenticeships, workshops, lecture series, and so forth) do we offer to the general student? What kind of commitment has our department made to the liberal education of all students?

6. Most of us would argue that our discipline is basic. But can we explain what is basic about our discipline? How has our program defined itself in terms of what is basic or fundamental to a liberal education and what is basic and fundamental to our discipline?

7. How is our academic unit perceived on campus by the faculty and by the administration? Are we considered intellectual leaders in communication and media studies and sense-makers of the communication/information age? Are we considered partners in the liberal arts? Do we consider it important to be considered campus leaders in communication, media studies and/or the liberal arts? If not, what academic units on campus are providing these functions?

8. Assuming we are always in the process of developing and fine-tuning our mission does our mission statement:
   a. contain a formulation of our goals and objectives that enables progress toward them to be measured?
   b. differentiate our program from other programs at the university and possibly other universities?
   c. define the "business" we want to be in?
   d. allow us to be establish priorities that are relevant to our stakeholders?
   e. describe how we plan to serve our stakeholders?
   f. excite and inspire, especially, faculty and students?
   g. reflect the educational philosophy of our program?

9. If we weren't preparing students for entry level jobs, would we still have a justification for existing?

10. What is the relationship we should foster with practitioners?

APPENDIX B: MISSION STATEMENTS LINKAGE
TO THE ASSESSMENT PLAN

1. Identify mission and purposes

a. Mission of school.

b. Mission of program.

c. Mission of journalism and mass communications.

d. Mission of education in journalism and mass communications.

e. Confirm core values, competencies, and knowledge.

f. Link specific values, competencies, and knowledge to outcomes.

g. Link curriculum to outcomes.

h. Link courses to curriculum to outcomes (outcome statement on each syllabus).

i. Within courses, link specific course units, exercises, and experiences to outcomes.

   1. Awareness (Knowledge): Lowest-level category, involves the remembering or recall of specifics. Key words: To define, recall, recognize. Sample test plan: Define "media censorship."

   2. Understanding (Comprehension): A low level of understanding, including acts of translating, interpreting, and extrapolation. Ideas are not related to one another. Key words: To translate, transform, state in one's own words. Sample test plan: Can properly interpret the use of three-point lighting.

   3. Application (Application): The use of abstraction to perform in a new situation. Key words: To generalize, relate, organize, classify. Sample test plan: Can use the criteria of the "Central Hudson Gas & Electric" case to support the banning of alcohol advertising.

   4. Analysis: Breaking down the elements of a situation and clarifying the rankings or relations among the elements. Key words: To distinguish, detect, discriminate, contrast. Sample test plan: Can identify differing motives of producers, advertisers, citizen groups, and audiences in the production of media texts.

   5. Synthesis: Combining elements to constitute a new pattern or structure. Key words: To produce, modify, restructure, originate, derive. Sample test plan: Can develop a 1-min news report explaining the constitutional grounds for a recent Supreme Court decision (adapted from Whitney, 1970, p. 3, and Erwin, 1991, pp. 39–40).

2. Determine best method to assess outcomes.

   a. Direct methods: Entry-level testing, sectional and departmental exams, capstone courses, portfolio assessment.

   b. Indirect methods: Grade distribution, student retention and graduation, probation and dismissal, internships and placement, stu-

TOURO COLLEGE LIBRARY

dent performance in local, regional, and national contests, student surveys and exit interviews, and alumni surveys (ACEJMC, 2004).

3. Results need to provide feedback into the system and be continuous.